A CAREER AS A

DIESEL MECHANIC

A CAREER AS A

DIESEL MECHANIC

JENNIFER CULP

Rosen
YA™
New York

Published in 2019 by The Rosen Publishing Group, Inc.
29 East 21st Street, New York, NY 10010

First Edition

Library of Congress Cataloging-in-Publication Data

Names: Culp, Jennifer, 1985– author.
Title: A career as a diesel mechanic / Jennifer Culp.
Description: New York : Rosen Publishing, 2019. | Series: Jobs for rebuilding America | Audience: Grades 7–12. | Includes bibliographical references and index.
Identifiers: LCCN 2017052859| ISBN 9781508179856 (library bound) | ISBN 9781508179863 (pbk.)
Subjects: LCSH: Diesel motor—Maintenance and repair. | Diesel motor industry—Vocational guidance.
Classification: LCC TJ795 .C75 2019 | DDC 621.43/68023—dc23
LC record available at https://lccn.loc.gov/2017052859

Manufactured in the United States of America

CONTENTS

Your day begins around 8:00 a.m. First, you check all your tools and make sure you have everything you need prepared for the day's jobs. It's important to have all the necessary tools and parts ready to go because truck drivers and fleet managers might be waiting on repairs so they can make deliveries on schedule. When it's time to start the job, you clock in—many shops ask their technicians to keep a record of hours per job so that the customer is billed fairly.

But new work doesn't stop rolling in while you're on the clock; a big part of working

The hard work of diesel mechanics keeps trucks on the road and keeps the economy of the United States rolling. Diesel mechanics are needed for many other kinds of vehicles and industrial machinery, too.

Diesel engines are built for durability and long wear. Diesel fuel provides more bang for the buck and hence is still extremely popular compared to unleaded fuels.

as a successful diesel mechanic is prioritizing time and balancing tasks so that all repairs get completed in a timely fashion. For instance, you might perform maintenance on a delivery truck that needs to be back up and running on a tight schedule before performing a repair on a private individual's pickup truck. You might clock out for a lunch break; or if you've got a particularly urgent job lined up, you might work straight through and grab a bite when you've finished.

The workday should end around 5:00 p.m., barring a last-minute emergency job. Overtime is common in this line of work, though, warn industry professionals. On the bright side, overtime means more money. At the end of the day, it's time to make an inventory of parts and tools for the next day so you'll be prepared for the new jobs on tomorrow's docket.

Alternatively, a typical day as a diesel mechanic could look entirely different. One could be called out to perform fieldwork at a construction site. It could mean days working at a marina or even months maintaining huge engines in a colossal engine room on a big ship out at sea.

Diesel technicians and mechanics inspect and repair any type of equipment with a diesel engine, including buses, trucks, agricultural and construction equipment, and marine vessels. Diesel mechanics perform routine maintenance, such as oil changes, and diagnose and repair failed components. Diesel repairs can involve fixing a vehicle's electrical system or doing major engine fixes. Diesel mechanics also work to retrofit older, updating them to more contemporary emission control systems and standards. Technicians in this line of work can be employed with trucking companies, state and local governments, agricultural and construction equipment dealers, marinas, and even motor vehicle and parts wholesalers. Anywhere there's a diesel engine, diesel mechanics are needed to keep it in good shape.

CHAPTER ONE

POWERED BY DIESEL: KEEPING THE COUNTRY RUNNING

Think about what you ate for dinner last night. Maybe you went to a restaurant. Have you ever wondered how a restaurant gets the ingredients the staff uses to prepare your meal? Or maybe you ate something prepared at home, using food bought at a grocery store. How does the store stay stocked with food? Do you use a car to go to and from the store? Cars run on gasoline that you buy at a gas station. But how did the gas get to the station in the first place? How about the clothes you're wearing? Unless you made them yourself, they were probably manufactured elsewhere and delivered by truck to the store where you bought them. Even if you did make your own clothes, the fabric you used was delivered to a store by another truck.

Food is delivered to grocery stores and restaurants by truck. Gasoline is delivered to gas stations by truck. Trucks deliver raw materials to manufacturers. Trucks deliver shipped goods in every category that exists. "If you bought it, a truck brought it," the saying goes, and in the domestic United States, the entire economy is dependent on the trucking industry. Even goods that are carried by airplanes, trains, and ships eventually travel on trucks to reach their final destinations. Without trucks to carry goods from place to place, the entire trade system would grind to a sudden halt.

The trucks that keep the economy moving aren't pickup trucks, but huge, heavy-duty diesel trucks, the eighteen-wheelers you see while traveling on interstates. These machines aren't cared for by personal auto mechanics, but by diesel mechanics with special skills developed to tend to long-haul equipment. These mechanics work day, night, and even on weekends to keep

A parking lot full of FedEx trucks sits ready to start the day's delivery shifts. Logistics companies like FedEx, and many other businesses and government agencies, require the work of diesel mechanics to keep goods moving.

their enormous charges in optimal functioning condition. Diesel truck technicians' work is vital: a problem with a transport truck could cause a wide-reaching delay in supply chain management or even cost lives in an accident. Without the labor of diesel mechanics, the whole country would slowly grind to a halt.

Trucking isn't the only industry that relies on the knowledge and skill of diesel mechanics. Vehicles and heavy construction equipment like bulldozers and cranes are powered by diesel engines, as are large commercial boats, passenger vehicles like buses, heavy-duty pickup trucks, military vehicles, and even

Diesel technicians work with an enormous variety of tools. Each job may bring unexpected challenges, and learning to analyze and solve problems is yet another useful tool in a mechanic's kit.

airplanes. Maintenance for these machines isn't just about the engine itself these days: as technology improves, many engines use electronics systems to control their operation, requiring mechanics to use computers to identify and fix problems with functionality. A mechanic might work specifically on electrical systems, the drive train (the system that delivers power to the wheels), the heating ventilation and air conditioning system (HVAC), the suspension system, or steering.

On a ship, diesel mechanics are responsible for monitoring boilers, generators, and pumps. Diesel mechanics may be called upon to make major engine repairs or to retrofit older engines with emission control systems to comply with modern antipollution regulations. They work with welding equipment, gas-powered pneumatic wrenches, lathes and grinding machines, in addition to hand tools such as hammers, pry bars, and every variety of wrenches.

DIESEL ON BOARD

Teams of diesel mechanics called ship engineers even work on cruise ships, traveling onboard for months at a time. Ship mechanics require a bachelor's degree in marine technology from a college or maritime academy, during which time they spend at least one semester at sea gaining hands-on experience working on a functioning ship and putting their education in thermodynamics, electrical engineering, gas turbines, hydraulics, ship systems, engineering mechanics, and instrumentation to practical use.

THE EYES AND HANDS

Dave, a diesel technician with Truck Center Companies, spoke of his experience working as a diesel mechanic since 2004 in an interview with DieselTechs.com. While earning his associate's degree from Universal Technical Institute in Phoenix, Arizona, his favorite course was Hot Rod U: "We built and tuned different combinations of components to see what worked and what didn't, it surprised us sometimes."

After more than ten years on the job, Dave appreciates the variety of work that comes with being a diesel tech. His least favorite aspect of working as a diesel tech is fixing flywheel housings and oil leaks underneath trucks—the literal dirty part of the job.

In his interview, Dave explained what makes diesel mechanics so vital to the trucking industry:

"No matter how much engineering, testing, and retesting the truck manufacturers put into their products they still break down. Until we get to the point that there are robot repairmen on the side of the road ready to fix any time of any day they will need a tech with his or her hands on the truck. We are the eyes and hands that fix what ships."

Furthermore, cruise ship mechanics require proper merchant mariner credentials to work at sea. The Transportation Worker Identification Credential is a United States Coast Guard federal requirement necessitating proof of citizenship, maritime training documentation, proof of sea experience, positive charater references, and a clean drug test and successful medical examination. Upon completion of the background check, prospective marine engineers must pass merchant mariner credentials engineering exams, which ensure adequate knowledge of control engineering, electronics, engineering safety, and environmental protection, along with diesel propulsion engines. Once this is accomplished, an applicant receives a position endorsement of third assistant engineer and is then legally certified to work on an commercial cruise ship.

WHAT'S THE DIFFERENCE WITH DIESEL?

Diesel engines actually predate the common use of gasoline engines like the ones in modern cars. In a gasoline engine, a spark ignites the fuel mixture that powers the vehicle. In a diesel engine, a piston compresses and heats the air in the engine, then fuel is sprayed in and ignited by the temperature of the combustion chamber. Unlike gasoline engines, diesel engines do not require a complicated electrical ignition and can also run on a greater variety of fuels than gasoline engines, even alternative fuels. They are generally less prone to malfunction

Diesel engines don't reside only in big trucks and construction equipment, but also in power boats, huge cargo ships, and even generators for facilities such as hospitals and government buildings.

"YOU FIGURE IT OUT"

In an interview with the Clark College Foundation, thirty-eight-year-old Nancy Boyce revealed the secret to her career success: "When you're a field mechanic, you can never say 'no.' You figure it out." Boyce enrolled in the diesel technician program at Clark College after layoffs from previous jobs at a textile mill and paper mill. Upon graduating, she was hired by a Caterpillar dealership in Portland, Oregon. After two years, she did some research to find the highest-paying Caterpillar dealership in the country: it was located in Juneau, Alaska, a place way to challenge herself where people depend on diesel generators for their livelihoods and even lives, she thought. She became the first woman Caterpillar diesel mechanic in the state.

Once when she dropped in to borrow a wrench from a local diesel mechanic college program in an emergency, the professor asked her to speak to the two female students in class. "I'm making $100 an hour right now, I'll see you later," she said as she grabbed the necessary socket wrench and left the classroom to the students' cheers. Today, Boyce runs her own company, PowerTech Generation, and employees three diesel techs other than herself to keep up with demand. Though fixing engines satisfies her, the most fulfilling part of her work is the difference she makes in the lives of people who depend on her labor. "It feels like what I was meant to do," she said.

than gasoline engines and are often used to power generators in emergency power systems for hospitals and government buildings. Widely regarded to be safer than gasoline, diesel fuel is less flammable than gasoline and will not form a potentially explosive mixture with the air if vaporized.

Diesel engines became a little more complicated after the 1970s, when the US government started to focus on reducing vehicular pollution. Emission control systems incorporate electronic fuel injection technology and computer-based pollution control measures, which means that modern diesel

Working on diesel engines isn't just for men. Anyone with mechanical aptitude and persistent determination to solve problems is a good candidate for training to become a diesel mechanic.

mechanics must possess a thorough knowledge of computer technology as it applies to engine operation and maintenance. Today's diesel mechanics also use a variety of electronic diagnostic systems to identify and repair various engine problems.

Prior to the incorporation of computer technology into diesel engines, many diesel mechanics received their training on the job. Now, most diesel technicians receive formal training through a community college or vocational training program. As an added benefit, receiving formal training provides an official record of a diesel mechanic's experience and knowledge. However, because there are no state or federal licensure requirements, an aspiring diesel mechanic has a lot of freedom in deciding exactly what training program is right for their individual needs. Diesel mechanics may become accredited specialists in one or more specific fields by passing examinations offered by the National Institute for Automotive Service Excellence (ASE). ASE certifies only mechanics who have a record of on-the-job experience or extensive formal training, and their various certifications make diesel technicians more competitive for job opportunities, especially those with higher pay.

CHAPTER TWO

WHAT DOES IT TAKE?

Manual dexterity is a must-have skill for diesel mechanics—that is, being good with your hands. Steady hands and good hand-eye coordination allow a diesel tech to work with both large tools and small, delicate parts. Sometimes diesel mechanics have to use their hands to keep parts steady or handle parts that may even be hard to see inside an engine. The job is quite literally hands on, so a level of comfort with manipulating engine components by hand is necessary. A good diesel mechanic might start out with a natural talent for working with his or her hands, but a persistent mechanic is even better. Practice makes perfect.

Mechanical aptitude is another qualification for a prospective diesel mechanic—it allows him or her to feel familiar and at ease with the workings of a complicated engine. This skill might also come easily to some people, while others need to work harder to familiarize themselves with the workings of various types of engines. Working with small engines can give someone hoping to eventually work with big engines a head start. Both Nancy Boyce, a mechanic who was

Hands-on education is vital for prospective diesel technicians. Tackling that first diesel engine on the job will feel like second nature after attending a thorough diesel repair educational program.

interviewed by Lily Raff McCaulou for Clark College Foundation, and Samantha Meinholz, a mechanic who was interviewed by Faith Hughes for *The Clarion*, the student publication of Madison Area Technical College, in Madison, Wisconsin, grew up on farms working with large farm equipment. Their comfort with mechanical machinery led them both to successful careers as working diesel mechanics. "I've always been around motors and stuff my whole life," said Ryan Schusted, a mechanic interviewed by Vicki Ikeogu for the *St. Cloud Times*. "I've raced snowmobiles and have done motocross. So I've always been around that kind of stuff."

WHAT DIESEL MECHANICS DO

Diesel technicians work with mechanical and electrical systems in order to find and resolve problems within each. Increasingly, diesel mechanics make use of computer diagnostic programs to identify issues in all aspects of an engine. Diesel techs do heavy work, lifting large parts and tools, and also make use of small precision equipment and hand tools like pliers, wrenches, and drills.

Diesel mechanics do preventative maintenance on diesel engines—tasks like tune-ups, wheel alignment, and brake adjustments—in order to keep everything running smoothly as expected. They also perform total rebuilds on engines that require it, taking every element apart for cleaning and replacement if necessary. Any task, no matter how small or large, that affects the proper running of a diesel engine falls under a diesel technician's purview. It could be an electrical short, a physical component that's worn out, even a computer problem. Any task required to maintain or repair a diesel engine is a diesel mechanic's job.

A diesel mechanic may use heavy equipment, such as a hydraulic lift, in conjunction with small hand-held tools, like wrenches and screwdrivers, in order to fix engines.

Diesel mechanics work in all kinds of locations and conditions. Many diesel technicians work in a shop environment, but others work on farms, construction sites, at marinas, on ships, or anywhere a fixed diesel generator needs repair. A diesel mechanic might even be called out to the side of a busy interstate to fix a vehicle that requires emergency repair. Wherever there are diesel engines, diesel technicians are needed to provide maintenance and repair.

Because diesel engines are expensive to replace, they are rebuilt at regular intervals, usually after a vehicle has traveled for more than 100,000 miles (about 160,000 kilometers) or an engine has operated for a certain number of hours. Mechanics take the engines completely apart, clean the components and replace worn parts, and put the engines back together.

"ALWAYS AROUND MOTORS"

As he recounted in a 2017 interview with the *St. Cloud Times*, twenty-three-year-old diesel mechanic Ryan Schusted grew up around the trade. Both his father and uncle worked in the construction industry using large diesel machinery. Growing up, he also raced motocross and snowmobiles in his home state of

(continued on the next page)

(continued from the previous page)

Minnesota, giving him a familiarity with motors and engines. After graduating from Cambridge-Isanti High School, Schusted landed a job in a truck shop in East Bethel, where he began to enjoy the variety and challenge of the work.

"I started to learn the ropes there," he said. "I don't know, I just liked it. I liked the idea that you could come into work and you don't know what you're going to be working on that day." After a year of working in the shop, he went to school at St. Cloud Technical & Community College to earn a degree in diesel mechanics. Classes in general service, diesel engines, hydraulics, electrical, and HVAC were structured so that Schusted and the other students spent mornings in the shop and afternoons in the classroom.

While still in school, he was hired by Freightliner of St. Cloud to maintain and repair heavy- and medium-duty trucks, starting with simple services such as brake jobs, oil changes, wheel seals, and minor electrical repair. Now he works on all aspects of the trucks and interacts with customers in the shop as a service writer. Schusted intends to work within the diesel industry until retirement, eventually doing full-time service writing and perhaps eventually becoming a foreman or service manager.

DIGITAL MEETS DIESEL

Technological aptitude allows for comfort in working with electronic and computer-controlled systems. Once again, learning how to effectively operate electronic and computer-based systems seems very intuitive to some people, whereas it takes longer for others to master. Patience and persistence are key.

Diagnosing nearly every problem requires the use of a laptop, said Ryan Schusted. All the necessary codes and tests are available through software, as are diagnostic tests and lists

What may look like a confusing and intimidating mess of wire and components to the layperson is familiar as the nervous system of an engine to an experienced diesel technician.

of steps to check for problems. "You can actually look up the codes and you can do all kinds of tests on there. As far as updating the software, nowadays, the new Freightliners have between seven and 10 different modules on the trucks that run them, and each of them have their own software," says Schusted. "Each time the factory finds a problem and they have to change something, they come out with a new software update and then when the trucks come in we update them," he explains.

Problem-solving skills are paramount for diesel mechanics, who may encounter unexpected challenges in the field, and both physical and mental stamina are necessary to endure the rigors of the job. According to an interview with the Clark College Foundation, mechanic Nancy Boyce spent a week fixing an excavator, garbage truck, diesel generator, and rock crusher on her first job working for Caterpillar at a logging camp in the city of Craig. Unable to return to her home in Juneau, Alaska, due to the weather, Boyce worked around the clock, taking naps on the treads of the rock crusher when she didn't have time to return to her hotel room. "Probably at 10 different times on that trip, I felt like I would die," she recounted ruefully, but instead she finished all of the jobs successfully by deadline and found herself hooked on the challenge. "It has become my addiction. Whether you are fixing a freighter's marine diesel or a Freightliner's OTR diesel, time is money in the world of diesel engine repair and heavy equipment technology. You need to have a strong knowledge base and use your sharp mind to diagnose and repair equipment," she explained. Clear-headed, quick thinking can spare a diesel technician a lot of trouble on the job.

"THE BEST FEELING THAT YOU CAN HAVE"

The student newspaper for Madison Area Technical College, *The Clarion*, featured the story of Samantha Meinholz, who landed a job working with semi trucks while she was still in the school's diesel technology program in 2011. Hiring took nine months, and with "a lot of pushing" on her part, Meinholz got a permanent job with Peterbilt before graduating in 2012. The company even built a special locker room to accommodate her as she was the first woman on the diesel tech team. Though the job isn't easy, Meinholz appreciated the welcoming attitudes of her more experienced male coworkers, who she says made a point to be kind and respectful.

Upon graduation, she joined the Peterbilt team full time. "The satisfaction of fixing equipment is the best," explained Meinholz, who had no prior experience working with diesel technology before she began the diesel program at Madison College. "When you pull up beside it or see it out on the road, and know that you fixed it, it's the best feeling that you can have.

GREEN DIESEL

A statement from the Association of Diesel Specialists (ADS) emphasizes the organization's commitment to the future of clean diesel as part of an environmental solution to global greenhouse gas issues. The ADS believes in the future of the inherently more efficient clean diesel power plant as a method of reducing our dependence on fossil fuels, and since diesel engines are capable of running on alternative fuels, the diesel industry finds itself in a unique position to advance this cause. The organization applauds the work of engine manufacturers in their efforts to continuously

Antipollution efforts are a part of diesel technicians' work. They are charged with ensuring that emissions control policies are followed correctly.

reduce emissions in diesel engines to near infinitesimal levels and believes that the use of clean diesel will improve the sustainability of consumers, businesses, and communities by reducing the environmental and societal cost of their activities.

The ADS opposes the use of devices made to intentionally contravene emission controls for use in equipment or vehicles used on a regular basis, believing that intentionally bypassing or altering emission controls in the name of performance enhancement undermines individual and group efforts to promote the use of clean diesel as a viable alternative power plan for the future. That gives the whole industry a bad name, and the field's professional organizations currently work to take diesel cleanly into the future.

THE CONTINUED DEMAND FOR DIESEL TECHNICIANS

The world needs more diesel mechanics. At the time of publication, there is currently a shortage of diesel-specific technicians to care for the diesel-powered industries of the United States. Older mechanics born in the baby boomer generation are retiring in great numbers, leaving jobs to be filled. Changing technologies in the industry mean that new recruits to the field must be skilled in computer diagnostics as well as engine maintenance and repair. America runs on diesel and requires talented technicians to keep the country's economic system moving. This need is beneficial to aspiring diesel mechanics, who have their pick of jobs!

In 2013, the head of Fire Fleet Services for the Los Angeles County Fire Department, in California, Division Chief Craig Weeks, said, "Across the board, the number-one maintenance issue for us is having a qualified pool of maintenance mechanics," in a roundtable interview for *Firehouse* magazine. Firehouses across the country require skilled diesel mechanics to reconcile aging fire truck engines with new emission control equipment— literally a matter of life and death, when it comes to reaching a fire scene when needed.

Ambulance services also employee diesel mechanics to keep their fleets in peak operable condition so that patient care is never interrupted by a breakdown. Hospitals' back-up power generators are powered by fixed diesel engines that require regular

It is imperative that emergency vehicles, such as ambulances and fire trucks, which run on diesel power, stay in good condition and ready to operate.

maintenance. America's emergency services run on diesel power, and diesel mechanics are a bit like medical specialists for diesel engines. "You pay what you need to pay to have that surgeon do the work," said fixed operations consultant Lloyd Schiller, likening diesel mechanics to neurosurgeons in an interview with *Automotive News* magazine, "It's brain surgery." Schiller went on to emphasize the technical aspect of the profession, noting that mechanics these days don't just replace components in the engine, but also hook their laptops up to each truck to replace the software.

The demand for diesel mechanics continues to grow. "As the stock of heavy vehicles and mobile equipment continues to increase, more service technicians will be needed to maintain them. In particular, demand for heavy equipment used in construction, mining, and energy exploration will result in employment growth for service technicians," the BLS reported in 2015. "There's such a shortage right now in diesel technicians that you can find jobs anywhere," diesel mechanic Ryan Schusted said in an interview with the *St. Cloud Times* in 2017.

Automotive dealerships, medium- and heavy-truck operations, agricultural equipment dealerships, oil-industry maintenance shops, the aerospace industry, and even cruise ships all compete for the services of skilled diesel technicians, and demand is not expected to slow any time soon. "About 50 percent of the people fixing cars and trucks right now are baby boomers. We're expected to lose about half of our workforce sometime in the next seven to 12 years to retirement. That's a big hole to fill," said Tony Molla of the National Institute for Automotive Service Excellence in 2015. "The outlook for qualified, especially high-end, diagnostic people is tremendous."

CHAPTER THREE

MECHANICS IN SCHOOL

So you're thinking of becoming a diesel mechanic, but you're still in high school. How can you best start preparing for your future career or maybe even get a head start? First and foremost: stay in school. You'll need a high school diploma or general education diploma in order to attend a diesel technology training program or secure employment at a reputable shop.

Material you learn in school can really help you become a stronger technician. Focus on math and sciences. "You will apply what you learned in math to help you analyze and solve problems like calculating gear ratios," says the National Automotive Technicians Foundation's literature for students. It adds, "Science, especially physics, is necessary to understand force, friction, hydraulics, and electrical circuits. And computerized engine management is spreading to trucks at lightning speed."

If there's any class that teaches basic electronics available at your school, take it. Shop classes are a huge boon to aspiring mechanics, offering an opportunity to become comfortable in a professional environment. Even if the only option available focuses primarily on gasoline engines, shop work will still familiarize you with engine systems and provide valuable hands-on experience working with real engine components.

Technology and related subjects in high school provide a good leg up when it comes to pursuing a technically challenging profession like that of diesel mechanic. Take as many shop, engineering, and other STEM-related courses as possible.

Computer familiarity is vital for today's diesel mechanics as well, so be sure to take advantage of your school's computers. School is vital for honing important professional skills, too. That's why students should be on time each day, dress neatly, and be respectful of their teachers and fellow students. Courtesy and good interpersonal skills are vital qualifications for diesel mechanics, who have to communicate with clients from all walks of life. School provides a place to practice workplace courtesy and collaboration, without the drastic consequences if you fail to meet the expectations of your employer (like getting fired).

Good customer service skills are important for diesel mechanics, who must be able to communicate with clients effectively.

Good time management is perhaps the most important skill in a technician's arsenal, as he or she must be able to effectively prioritize and balance the workload to keep every client satisfied. Furthermore, professionalism breeds mutual respect. A polite, organized, and timely diesel mechanic is likely to enjoy much more positive customer interactions than someone who dresses sloppily and arrives to work late.

"I ALWAYS LOVED HEAVY EQUIPMENT"

Mechanic Justin Britton, featured in an article on the mikeroweWORKS Foundation website, fell in love with big machines as a little kid visiting his father's workplace. His dad drove a bulldozer, and Britton also learned about large trucks from his mother, who worked as the manager of a truck scale house, weighing 80,000-pound (36,287-kilogram) commercial trucks for Clayton Sand Company in New Jersey.

When Britton's sophomore high school class took a field trip to visit the campus of Universal Technical Institute in Pennsylvania, his old interest in huge engines was rekindled.

"I always loved heavy equipment," he said. "Each year after that we would visit the school and my interest would grow stronger." In the summer before his senior year of high school, Britton got a job working at his mom's old employer, Clayton Sand, as a mechanic's helper, machine operator, and laborer, which gave him experience working with big machines and also helped him save to pay for his school tuition without going into heavy debt. He found that he really enjoyed the work, which assured him that his ambition to become a diesel mechanic was the right choice. And he garnered a scholarship through the mikeroweWORKS foundation to help with the cost.

SHADOW A PROFESSIONAL

Do research on businesses and organizations in your region that work on diesel engines. These can be found on the internet or via word of mouth. Call to arrange a visit. Shadowing professionals in action gives you a clear picture of what the job is actually like and also counts as experience that you can list on your application to a college or technical school. If you are a highly motivated individual, some shops might even hire you as an assistant prior to graduation, giving you real hands-on experience in your future work environment and a paycheck to boot.

Today, an apprenticeship is still a valuable way to learn and grow in expertise and the main way most younger workers advance in a trade like diesel service.

Justin Britton, a mechanic interviewed by the author, took a job working as a mechanics helper and laborer for a construction business in the summer between his junior and senior year of high school. After graduation and earning a certificate in a diesel technology training program in another state, he moved back home to take on greater responsibility working full-time as a heavy equipment technician for that same business.

Due to the dearth of much-needed diesel mechanics in the United States, opportunity abounds for people who want to work in the field. Corporate sponsors often partner with colleges and technical schools to partially or fully fund students' education, offering them guaranteed jobs upon completion of training. Do some research on diesel businesses and educational programs in your area. You're likely to find many hungry for applicants. Heavy equipment technician Jason Serfling took advantage of the Caterpillar ThinkBIG program at Lake Area Technical College to fund his education. He earned multiple tool-procurement scholarships, too. Today he works as a full-time CAT service technician in exchange for the investment the company made in his future.

As in any industry, networking and making contacts is vital to success. To gain the benefit of a mentor, instructors, potential employers, and friends in the industry, you have to reach out to meet some of them. Shadowing professionals in the field in which you're interested not only gives you an up-close-and-personal view of the job in action, but also demonstrates your enthusiasm and willingness to learn to potential employers and your coworkers.

"IT'S NEVER REPETITIVE!"

Jason Serfling is a full-time heavy equipment service technician for Butler Machinery Company in Rapid City, Michigan. "The thing I like the most about my work is the continuous change; it's never repetitive," he said in an interview with the mikeroweWORKS Foundation.

Serfling didn't enter the diesel industry immediately after graduating from high school. He worked as a welder in the US Navy for four years, including three years stationed in Sasabo, Japan. He continued to work as a welder for a year in Michigan after leaving the Navy, then transitioned to a job as a machinist, which he did for four years in Big Rapids, Michigan, while his wife attended optometry school. Following a move to South Dakota, Serfling realized he wanted a job with greater pay and benefits, and the diesel industry caught his eye.

The Caterpillar ThinkBIG program at Lake Area Technical College allowed him to get an education in his new field and train to become a CAT dealer service technician. In 2013, he graduated with honors as one of the top students in his class, and his high grades earned him tool procurement scholarships from the mikeroweWORKS Foundation, Butler Machinery Company, and Lake Area Technical Institute Foundation. "I enjoy the continuous learning about new technology and other advancements in our industry," he said. "I am happy with my position and look forward to improving my knowledge and skills."

A program that offers a small student-to-teacher ratio and a good balance of hands-on learning alongside classroom work is ideal for an aspiring diesel mechanic. Learning by doing is the quickest way to diesel expertise.

In an interview for Western Technical College's website, Fidel Gonzalez, a diesel vehicle repair business owner, said he hired one of his former classmates to work for him after graduation. "He knew what he was doing," Gonzalez explained of the decision. A good impression goes a long way, especially in a professional setting.

CHAPTER FOUR

BEGINNING A CAREER WITH BIG ENGINES

*P*rior to the founding of the National Institute for Automotive Service Excellence in the 1970s, most diesel mechanics learned their trade through on-the-job apprenticeship. In this method of entering the field, inexperienced would-be diesel mechanics work as assistants to experienced technicians and learn how to maintain and repair diesel engines through observing and helping with tasks. As the trainee's skills improve, he or she is entrusted with increasingly complicated jobs until eventually he or she is able to diagnose and repair problems alone and becomes a fully fledged diesel mechanic.

This practice has the advantage of offering the candidate a wealth of hands-on experience. However, it also comes with limitations: with only on-the-job training, fledgling diesel technicians receive training only in tasks that come into the shop, rather than learning about many potential problems that may arise. Furthermore, this practice has fallen out of favor with most employers, who prefer to hire workers with formal training and even certification.

Though there are no federal educational or certification requirements in place to become a working diesel mechanic, due

Classroom success is as important as mechanical aptitude. If you want to become a diesel mechanic in the future, work hard to obtain your high school diploma or GED.

to legal reasons most employers require that anyone hired as a diesel mechanic be at least eighteen years of age. Additionally, most employers prefer that their mechanics hold either a high school diploma or a General Education Development (GED) certification, which is also a requirement to earn an associate's degree or attend a diesel-specific vocational training program. Furthermore, a high school education provides aspiring diesel mechanics with a solid math and science background so they can understand complex subjects like diesel engine controls and fuel injection systems. Some community colleges or vocational schools

DIESEL DREAMS

An online alumnus profile published by the Central Wisconsin Workforce Development Board details the diesel success story of Lindsay Huffman. Ever since she was a little girl, Huffman knew knew she wanted to be a diesel mechanic like her father. Tragically, he passed away when she was a senior in high school. Through her grief, she enlisted the help of a friend and continued to work on her senior project of rebuilding a Cummins 3.9-liter diesel engine, dedicating the project to her dad's memory.

After graduation, Huffman turned to the Workforce Investment Act Adult Program for assistance. Through the program, she was assigned a caseworker who helped her develop an employment plan that offered tuition assistance. At Nicolet College and then Fox Valley Technical College in Wisconsin, Huffman worked hard and earned a spot on the dean's list every semester. She worked summers with Fox Valley's Girl Tech program, mentoring more than seventy young women interested in the field.

Huffman graduated with an associate degree with high honors as a diesel technician and only one month later attained a job working as a diesel mechanic for Bowen's Bus Service in Rhinelander, Wisconsin. Today, Huffman lives her childhood dream of working to maintain and repair huge engines, just like her father before her.

may even allow a student to enter a diesel-engineering program while he or she is still working to obtain an equivalency degree.

Traditional college programs that provide a bachelor's degree last four years. Most college-based diesel programs offer associate's degrees, which may be completed in two years. Some schools, such as the University of Northwest Ohio, for example, offer both two-year and four-year associate and bachelor's degrees in diesel technology. Technical and trade schools may also offer shorter sessions that provide particular diesel specialty certificates in a matter of weeks. As in most occupations, more education tends to provide more career opportunities and higher paychecks.

TOP TEN TIPS

The National Automotive Technicians Foundation (NATEF) is a nonprofit organization associated with the National Institute for Automotive Service Excellence (ASE). Just as ASE certifies professional diesel mechanics to ensure high quality of service, NATEF accredits diesel technology programs in schools in order to improve the quality of diesel training programs nationwide. Therefore, NATEF certification is a good benchmark for prospective students to look for in a program: a program with NATEF certification knows what the industry is about and is guaranteed to prepare students for a bright future working on big engines.

NATEF provides a number of resources for aspiring diesel technicians, including an easy search tool to find accredited

After-school technology clubs are a great place to have fun and challenge your technical skills in a supportive and friendly environment.

schools (available on their website at natef.org). The organization also offers helpful advice for choosing the right school and beginning a career or continuing one's education. NATEF's Top Ten Tips, sourced from ASE-certified master technicians, are particularly appropriate to consider:

1. Education, Education, Education. A solid foundation in math, reading, study skills, computer skills, and electronics is necessary for a good diesel technician.

2. Take advantage of on-the-job training, co-op, or apprenticeship opportunities. Many schools partner with professional industry organizations to place students in part-time work while still in school, which can provide a student with both a paycheck and valuable hands-on experience before he or she graduates into the full-time workforce.

3. Keep abreast of new technology. As tech changes and evolves, successful mechanics continue educating themselves to stay on top of current trends.

4. Learn a systems approach. This kind of approach focuses on the overall interaction of mechanical and electronic components within an engine, which helps a technician assess and solve problems even in unfamiliar complex engines, rather than getting hung up on working with a single specific type of engine, which limits opportunity.

5. Develop good communication skills. As NATEF notes, "Your credibility is linked to your perceived competence."

6. Keep a positive attitude. If you enjoy doing the work thoroughly, you'll always do a good job!

7. Take pride in your work. Likewise, if you're proud of the job you do, you'll do it well. Master technicians advise working on every vehicle as if you own it personally.

8. Be honest and ethical. Dependability keeps customers coming back.

9. Cultivate professionalism in yourself and others. Be competent, be timely, and take pride in appearance and cleanliness.

10. Become ASE certified. This may seem like predictable advice from ASE-certified master technicians, perhaps, but it's still important—ASE certification is the national standard of excellence in the United States and leads to better job opportunities and higher pay.

CHAPTER FIVE

FROM SCHOOL TO THE WORKPLACE

Before choosing a diesel technician training program, you need to make sure it's a good one. First, check to make sure a school is accredited by the Accrediting Commission of Career Schools and Colleges of Technology or Accrediting Council for Independent Colleges and Schools. Both are national accrediting agencies recognized by the United States Department of Education. Employers may accept training from an unaccredited program, but it's best to be on the safe side. The next thing to consider in selecting a training program is the teacher to student ratio. Will you get enough personalized attention from the instructor? You don't want to choose a program in which the teacher is overwhelmed by an overly large class.

You should also consider teacher credentials when choosing a program. How much experience in the diesel industry do the teachers really have? Does the school have a good reputation for placing students into jobs? These factors should help you decide whether to apply for and spend money on the program. If you don't know anyone personally who has attended a program, consult online reviews.

Prospective diesel mechanics need strong math and mechanical skills to succeed in their chosen field. Nurturing one's curiosity and working hard in school will benefit any aspiring diesel mechanic.

Modern facilities and up-to-date equipment are a must to prepare you to work with cutting edge technology. Of course, the program should also prepare you to work with old technology that has yet to be updated or needs to be integrated with new equipment to meet contemporary safety standards. Industry partnerships allow students to learn how to work with current technologies in the field deployed by companies such as Rockwell, Cummins, Mack, Spicer, Caterpillar, Ziegler, Inc., and others. As such, they are a great school-to-work pipeline.

A good school comes equipped with all of the tools you need to learn how to be an effective diesel mechanic and may even, through partnerships, offer a program to allow students to acquire their own tools affordably.

The College of Alameda in California, for example, maintains numerous industry partnerships with organizations, corporations, and municipal institutions. These relationships put students ahead of the game, not only providing them with access to up-to-date tools and technologies, but also allowing pupils to develop familiarity with the organizations they will need to interact with as professionals in the field. Both Caterpillar and Peterson Tractor & Power Systems even award grants that fund scholarships for qualified students to help defray the costs of the program.

"I COULDN'T HAVE DONE IT WITHOUT HELP"

As explained in *CORD*, the publication of the Southwest Wisconsin Workforce Development Board, forty-year-old Craig Bunker entered the diesel technology field in a nontraditional fashion. He had been out of school for more than twenty years when he was laid off from his job at Lear Seating, putting him out of work with a family to support. However, he saw an opportunity to improve his situation by going to school to become a diesel mechanic, which typically pays better than regular automotive work. While attending Blackhawk Technical College, he started working part time for a diesel operation in Wisconsin called Smooth Operators, Inc.

After earning his degree, he switched to working on heavy trucks full time. Though returning to school for training proved challenging for Bunker, having a job waiting when he finished the program served as a light at the end of a trying tunnel. "I couldn't have gone back to school without help," he said. "I may be looking to advance in the future, but for now I'm happy with this job at Smooth Operators and I plan to give them the best I have. I'm just thankful and excited about the support I received."

GETTING HANDS ON

One of the most important considerations in choosing a program is the amount of time allotted for hands-on learning in addition to classroom lessons. Working as a diesel mechanic means working with your hands, and there's no other way to adequately learn how to do so than actually doing the work. A reputable program will offer a lot of time in the garage to supplement learning from books in the classroom, and a quality instructor will be comfortable working with his or her hands in an engine.

One of the service branches of the US military is a great place to get quality training working on mechanical systems. Of course, it is a big commitment to enlist and fulfill one's obligations in exchange for that expertise.

"I LIKE GETTING DIRTY"

When Samantha Brumley joined the Army as a communications specialist at age seventeen, she really wanted to become a medic, according to Army First Sergeant Kevin Hartman's article, "Face of Defense: Female Tank Mechanic Likes Dirty Work" published by the U.S. Department of Defense (DOD) Instead, Brumley found work as an armament repairer who fixed and maintained weapons systems.

When a 2013 decision by the Pentagon opened up combat roles to women, Brumley was asked if she would like to go to school to become a tank mechanic. Her response was matter of fact: "I'm not a desk-type person. I like getting hands-on. I like getting dirty. So I was like 'Yeah, I wanna go,'" she said. In 2014, she became the first woman to attend the tank mechanics course at the Regional Training Institute in Umatilla, Oregon. "I'm proud of being the first female tank mechanic, but I don't like getting called out on it because it's different," Brumley said. "It's just a job and an opportunity," she explained. When Brumley eventually leaves the armed forces, she has her civilian career planned out: "I want to be a diesel mechanic!" she said. "I want to work on stuff."

Learning on the job was once how every diesel mechanic learned the skills of the trade. Today, hands-on learning is a vital element of diesel technician training. Furthermore, some schools, particularly those with industry partnerships, may be able to help students acquire expensive tools of the trade at reduced cost while they are still in training. Due to the nationwide shortage of diesel technicians and cooperation from industry operations, many schools can also help set students up with paying jobs while they are still working to earn their degree.

In a 2016 interview with the *West Fargo Pioneer*, Zachary Lyon, a high school graduate, discussed how he signed up for the Komatsu Diesel Tech Program while enrolled at North Dakota State College of Science in Wahpeton, North Dakota. The program not only netted him an internship at General Equipment and Supplies, but also pays for the bulk of his college tuition and guarantees him a full-time job upon graduation. "I wanted to pursue diesel mechanics. In West Fargo [High School], I took a class for engines, and I learned a lot of mechanics at home working on vehicles. I learned a lot. It's half learning from teachers and half from experience. I just always enjoyed to learn how everything works," Lyon explained. If he maintains a 3.6 grade point average throughout his time in school, General Equipment and Supplies will reimburse him for 100 percent of his college tuition costs upon graduation. "It's really nice and will really motivate you to pay attention and to do well," he said.

Another option for education in diesel technology is to join the military. "Overhauling engines. Repairing mechanical evaporators that turn seawater into freshwater. Troubleshooting systems on an F/A-18 Hornet. Without the skills of those working in the mechanical and industrial technology field, the Navy's technologically advanced machinery and equipment would be little more than a mass of wires and metal," states the US Navy's website.

Wheeled vehicle mechanics are also needed in the Army, and work as a Marine engineer equipment mechanics is considered a military occupation specialty with a rank range from private to staff sergeant. To qualify as an engineer equipment mechanic with the US Marines, a candidate must receive a mechanical maintenance score of 95 or above on the Armed Services Vocational Aptitude Battery test. Then, following basic training, Marine diesel mechanics receive training at the Marine detachment at the US Army Engineer School at Fort Leonard Wood, Missouri.

CHAPTER SIX

ASE AND OTHER CERTIFICATIONS

The National Institute for Automotive Service Excellence, known as ASE, is an independent nonprofit organization that was created in 1972. Its purpose is to improve quality in vehicle service and repair by testing and certifying automotive professionals in various specialties. Though there are no current federal certification requirements in place for employment as a diesel mechanic, in practice, many diesel mechanics receive formal training in their field.

ASE certification may be obtained by mechanics who have two years of on-the-job training or one year of professional automotive work along with a two-year degree in automotive repair to qualify for certification, ensuring that every ASE candidate is experienced prior to taking any ASE exam. Qualifications for necessary work experience may vary slightly between categories, so all applicants must submit their work histories for review by the institute prior to receiving approval to take one or more exams.

Passing one or more of the ASE examinations is one way that a mechanic demonstrates that he or she is qualified to perform his or her work to the highest standards.

ACING THE ASE EXAMINATIONS

ASE examinations are challenging. According to statistics reported by the National Institute for Automotive Service Excellence, only two out of three test takers pass their ASE certification test on the first try. The exams are different for each subspecialty: medium/heavy truck, truck equipment, school bus, collision repair, and many more. ASE offers certification in more than forty specific automotive and diesel specialty

"LET US TAKE CARE OF YOU"

A story featured on the website of his alma mater, Western Technical College, says that Fidel Gonzalez graduated with a diesel technology degree from Western Technical College in El Paso, Texas, in 2011 and opened his own business, Roadrunner Diesel and Transportation, in September of the very same year.

Gonzalez enjoyed his time in training to become a diesel technician; he particularly loved the feeling that comes with taking an engine apart and successfully putting it back together and the detail of knowing exactly what each part of the engine does.

Once Gonzalez started his own business, he even hired another Western Technical graduate to work for him: Andres Curier, who impressed Gonzalez with his confidence and skill in the classroom. "We handle all service from tires to repairs on everything from cars to tractors. We also do roadside service calls 24 hours a day and will even come to you and bring you and your vehicle back to the shop," he explained. "Our company motto is 'Let me and my crew take care of you.'"

fields, providing tangible proof of a mechanic's excellence in a particular area.

As of 2017, nearly 20,500 technicians in the United States are ASE certified in diesel engine repair and maintenance, but only 1,622 are certified in transit bus diesel engines and 2,102 in school bus diesel engines. If an individual earns certification in each of the following categories simultaneously—diesel engines, drive train, brakes, suspension and steering, electrical/electronic systems, and HVAC—he or she becomes certified as an ASE master medium-heavy vehicle technician.

Finding a mentor is another way to augment the hard work, extensive study, and significant hands-on job experience necessary to work as a diesel mechanic.

ASE certification, independently regulated, is a nationally recognized standard for quality in diesel mechanics. Certification offers diesel technicians specific proof of their skills and often leads to increased rates of pay. It also offers employers and customers peace of mind in reassurance of an individual mechanic's skill. If a certified technician wishes to maintain his or her status, he or she must pass another exam every five years. Pursuing this kind of certification demonstrates a big commitment to staying sharp and up to date with both knowledge and skill, but the reward is worth the hassle for many diesel technicians. "The real opportunities lie for those who have the most relevant training and tend to keep learning as they move through their career," said Tony Molla, vice president of communications with the National Institute for Automotive Service Excellence, in a 2015 article for the *Green Bay Press-Gazette*.

Individuals who are interested in marine diesel work are certified through the American Boat and Yacht Council (ABYC) in any of eight areas, including diesel engine and support systems. Master marine technician certification may be earned by passing any three of the eight exam subjects, which also cover electrical systems, marine corrosion, refrigeration and air conditioning, and even composite boat building. These certifications are helpful for anyone who wishes to specialize in marine diesel work, proving a technician's ability within the specialty.

Proper ASE certifications prove a mechanic's ability to work on cranes, earthmovers, and other heavy machines, but to build skill further a diesel technician who works on construction equipment may even choose to become certified to operate heavy equipment through the National Center for

Construction Education and Research (NCCER). Certification for heavy equipment operations allows a technician to work on equipment without relying on other operators, and familiarity with the mechanics from an operator's point of view can help a technician more precisely understand operator concerns and diagnose trouble.

Although ASE is the only independent accrediting organization for diesel mechanics in the United States, it is also possible to receive brand-specific certifications through corporations such as Caterpillar, Penske, and Ford. These certifications prepare a mechanic to work on the specific type of equipment produced by the company who provides certification. This approach may limit the scope of a diesel technician's field of work but provides near-guaranteed employment in working for a particular company's businesses.

THE ADS

The Association of Diesel Specialists (ADS) is not a certifying body, but the leading international organization of diesel industry professionals. According to its mission statement, the ADS aims to serve as a complete resource for training, technical service information, member promotion, and networking opportunities for professional diesel technicians. The network provided by ADS allows diesel mechanics from all over the world to share knowledge and access resources to improve their trade.

As mentioned elsewhere, the Association of Diesel Specialists is committed to advancing green diesel initiatives, encouraging members to embrace anti-pollution efforts. In this fashion, the organization hopes to advance the diesel industry safely and profitably into the future. Membership in the ADS may be a boon to professional diesel mechanics who wish to expand their professional networks and interact with fellow diesel technicians from all over the world.

THE OUTLOOK

The median income that diesel mechanics can expect to earn, even at the beginning of their careers, is considered to be a middle-class income; it is well above the minimum wage. According to literature provided by NATEF, beginning salaries of diesel mechanics are competitive, while experienced and senior mechanics and managers make decent wages. They can expect to make even more than their base wage with overtime or in out-of-the-way locations.

In 2014, there were 263,900 diesel service technicians and mechanics in the United States. The job outlook for the occupation is predicted to rise 12 percent between 2014 and 2024, faster than average. The Bureau of Labor Statistics (BLS) expects to see at least 31,600 more people employed in the industry by 2024. With the advent of computer systems and current emission control technology, the diesel industry is changing, but it's here to stay. Diesel power is more stable than gasoline and should continue to fuel the country's transport economy for years to come, requiring diesel mechanics to keep the country running.

THE DIESEL BROTHERS

Maybe you've watched real-life best friends "Heavy D" Sparks and "Diesel Dave" Kiley's reality television show on the Discovery Channel—in spite of the title, they're not actually blood relations. The "brothers" do run a real diesel business, however; their "DieselSellerz" social media accounts and free truck giveaways attracted so much attention that now they have their own show featuring pranks, sneaky science lessons, and a whole lot of fixing trucks. The Diesel Brothers started their business by buying old used and broken-down trucks and fixing them for resale.

In high school, Sparks studied auto mechanics, welding, and fabrication, and after graduation he began working at an all-terrain vehicle and motorcycle rental operation that allowed him to gain hands-on experience working with motors and engines. After one semester of college, he dropped out to operate heavy equipment for his uncle's construction business, which got him interested in bigger and bigger machines. Kiley came into the picture when Sparks accidentally put gasoline in his new diesel truck—Kiley helped syphon it out of the tank, and the rest is history. In 2010, the "brothers" founded DieselSellerz, which also employs "The Muscle," who "comes from a family of diesel fanatics," and "Redbeard," who grew up driving diesel trucks in his childhood home of the Uintah Basin, a part of a Ute Indian reservation. DieselSellerz did their first refurbished truck giveaway in 2013 and have given away more than twenty trucks since.

In addition to the show, the business includes an online truck parts store, an apparel company, a full service custom truck building shop and dealership, and a line of tires that Sparks developed specifically for use with diesel trucks. In 2017, Sparks and Kiley even published a book: *The Diesel Brothers: A Truckin' Awesome Guide to Trucks and Life.*

Television personalities the Diesel Brothers discuss their upcoming book on an episode of the web-based series *Build*.

- Diesel service technicians and mechanics inspect, repair, and overhaul buses and trucks or maintain and repair any type of diesel engine.

- Diesel service technicians and mechanics usually work in well-ventilated but often noisy repair shops. They occasionally repair vehicles on roadsides or at worksites. Most diesel technicians work full time, and overtime and evening shifts are common.

- Many diesel service technicians and mechanics learn informally on the job after a high school education, but employers increasingly prefer applicants who have completed postsecondary training programs in diesel engine repair. Although not required, industry certification can be important for diesel technicians.

- Employment of diesel service technicians and mechanics is projected to grow 12 percent from 2014 to 2024, faster than the average for occupations. Job opportunities should be best for those who have completed postsecondary training in diesel engine repair.

GLOSSARY

accredited Officially recognized or authorized by an examining body.

alternative fuel A fuel other than gasoline or diesel for powering motor vehicles, such as natural gas, methanol, or electricity.

aptitude A natural talent for something.

diesel engine An internal-combustion engine in which heat produced by the compression of air in the cylinder is used to ignite the fuel.

drive train The system in a motor vehicle that connects the transmission to the drive axles.

emission control The means employed to limit the discharge of noxious gases from the internal-combustion engine and other components.

flammable The quality of easily being set on fire.

fossil fuel A naturally occurring fuel such as coal or gas that is extracted from the earth and is made up of the long-gone remains of living things.

gasoline engine An internal-combustion engine that has its piston driven by explosions of a mixture of air and vapor of gasoline or another volatile fuel ignited by an electric spark.

generator A machine that converts mechanical energy into electricity.

HVAC An abbreviation for heating, ventilation, and air conditioning system.

hydraulics Systems powered by the conveyance of liquids through pipes and channels.

retrofit To add a component or an accessory to something that did not originally have it.

semi A large eighteen-wheeled transport truck, also known as a tractor trailer or big rig.

shadow To accompany a professional at work to observe his or her activities and learn that person's job duties.

shop Short for repair shop, refers to the facility in which technicians work to maintain and repair engines.

suspension The system of springs and shock absorbers by which a vehicle is cushioned from bumpy roads.

thermodynamics A branch of physics concerned with heat and temperature and their relation to energy and work.

Association of Diesel Specialists
400 Admiral Boulevard
Kansas City, MO 64106
(816) 285-0810
Website: http://diesel.org
The worldwide diesel industry's leading trade association,
the Association of Diesel Specialists is dedicated to
the highest level of service for diesel fuel injection and
related systems.

Canadian Diesel Online
Lloydminster, AB T9V 0W8
Canada
(855) 390-4932
Website: https://canadiandieselonline.ca
Facebook and Instagram: @canadiandieselonline
Canadian Diesel Online is the leading diesel components
supplier in Canada.

Diesel Technology Forum
5291 Corporate Drive, Suite 102
Frederick, MD 21703
(301) 668-7230
Website: http://www.dieselforum.org
Facebook and Twitter: @Dieseltechforum
The Diesel Technology Forum promotes cleaner diesel fuel,
advanced engines, and effective emissions control technology.

Internal Combustion Engine Division
American Society of Mechanical Engineers (ASME)
Mail Stop 23 S-1
3 Park Avenue
New York, NY 10016-5990
(212) 591-7123
Website: https://community.asme.org/internal_combustion
    _engine_division/default.aspx
Twitter: @asmedotorg
Facebook: @ASME.org
The Internal Combustion Engine Division of the ASME is
    devoted to the art and science of mechanical engineering
    of engines, encouraging and fostering research and
    development for mobile, marine, rail, generation, and
    stationary applications.

International Association of Machinists and
    Aerospace Workers
9000 Machinists Place
Upper Marlboro, MD 20772
(301) 967-4500
Website: https://www.goiam.org
Twitter: @MachinistsUnion
The IAM is a labor union that represents thousands of auto
    and truck technicians and mechanics in North America.

Natural Resources Canada
580 Booth Street, 15th floor
Ottawa, ON K1A 0E4

Canada
(343) 292-6100
Website: http://www.nrcan.gc.ca/home
Twitter: @NRCan
Natural Resources Canada provides information and guidance
    on safe energy sources in Canada.

US Bureau of Labor Statistics (BLS)
Postal Square Building
2 Massachusetts Avenue NE
Washington, DC 20212-0001
(202) 691-5200
Website: https://www.bls.gov
Twitter: @BLS_gov
The BLS is an agency within the US Department of
    Labor and measures labor market activity, working
    conditions, and price fluctuations in the economy. It
    collects, analyzes, and provides important economic
    information to the public. Its website contains the
    Occupational Outlook Handbook (https://www
    .bls.gov/ooh) that describes various jobs, working
    conditions, and salary data for numerous jobs,
    including diesel mechanics and related technicians.

Armantrout, Bob, and Lyle Estill. *Backyard Biodiesel: How to Brew Your Own Fuel.* Gabriola Island, BC: New Society Publishers, 2015.

Bell, Joseph. *Modern Diesel Technology: Electricity and Electronics.* Clifton Park, NY: Delmar Cengage Learning, 2013.

Bennett, Sean. *Modern Diesel Technology: Diesel Engines.* Clifton Park, NY: Delmar Cengage Learning, 2014.

Berwick, Dennison. *Marine Diesel Basics 1: Maintenance, Lay-up, Winter Protection, Tropical Storage, Spring Recommission.* Toronto, ON: Voyage Press, 2017.

Dixon, John. *Modern Diesel Technology: Heating, Ventilation, Air Conditioning & Refrigeration.* Clifton Park, NY: Delmar Cengage Learning, 2013.

Heavy D & Diesel Dave. *The Diesel Brothers: A Truckin' Awesome Guide to Trucks and Life.* New York, NY: Gallery Books, 2017.

Hesse, Tyson. *Tyson Hesse's Diesel: Ignition.* Burbank, CA: BOOM! Box, 2016.

Huzij, Robert, and Angelo Spano. *Modern Diesel Technology: Heavy Equipment Systems.* Clifton Park, NY: Delmar Cengage Learning, 2013.

Toboldt, William. *Diesel: Fundamentals, Service, Repair.* Tinley Park, IL: Goodheart-Willcox Pub, 1983.

Wright, Gus. *Fundamentals of Medium/Heavy Duty Diesel Engines.* Burlington, MA: Jones & Bartlett Learning, 2015.

BIBLIOGRAPHY

Advanced Technology Institute. "A Day in the Life of a Diesel Mechanic." December 1, 2015. https://www.auto.edu/blog/a-day-in-the-life-of-a-diesel-mechanic-salary-facts-figures.

Advanced Technology Institute. "What Are the Top Diesel Mechanic Certifications to Have?" November 3, 2015. https://www.auto.edu/blog/what-are-the-top-diesel-mechanic-certifications-to-have.

Ballam, Ed. "Fire & Rescue Apparatus Maintenance Roundtable." *Firehouse*, January 4, 2013. http://www.firehouse.com/article/10840191/fire-rescue-apparatus-maintenance-roundtable.

Bureau of Labor Statistics. "Occupational Outlook Handbook: Diesel Service Technicians and Mechanics." Retrieved September 25, 2017. https://www.bls.gov/ooh/installation-maintenance-and-repair/diesel-service-technicians-and-mechanics.htm.

Diesel Mechanic Guide. "Becoming a Cruise Ship Diesel Mechanic." Retrieved September 25, 2017. http://www.dieselmechanicguide.com/becoming-cruise-ship-diesel-mechanic.

Diesel Tech. "A Day in the Life of a Diesel Mechanic." March 22, 2016. https://www.dieseltechjobs.com/diesel-mechanic-news/a-day-in-the-life-of-a-diesel-mechanic-588.

DieselTechs.com. "Meet the Diesel Technician, Dave." Retrieved September 25, 2017. http://www.dieseltechs.com/meet-dave.html.

Discovery Channel. "About the Show: Diesel Brothers."
    Retrieved September 25, 2017. https://www.discovery
    .com/tv-shows/diesel-brothers/about.
Hartman, Kevin. "Face of Defense: Female Tank Mechanic
    Likes Dirty Work." US Department of Defense.
    Retrieved September 25, 2017. https://www.defense
    .gov/News/Article/Article/603128/face-of-defense
    -female-tank-mechanic-likes-dirty-work.
Hartmann, Joan. "Lindsey Huffman's Success Story."
    North Central Wisconsin Workforce Development
    Board. Retrieved September 25, 2017. http://ncwwdb
    .org/lindsey-huffmans-success-story.
Hughes, Faith. "Fixing Big Rigs: Only Female in Diesel
    Program Is Groundbreaker in Profession." *The Clarion*,
    February 22, 2012. https://www.theonlineclarion.com
    /news/2012/02/22/fixing-big-rigs-only-female-in
    -diesel-program-is-groundbreaker-in-profession.
Ikeogu, Vicki. "Childhood Hobby Turned into Career for
    Diesel Mechanic." *St. Cloud Times*, February 4, 2017.
    http://www.sctimes.com/story/news/local
    /spark/2017/02/04/childhood-hobby-turned-into
    -career-diesel-mechanic/96395124.
McCaulou, Lily Raff. "First Female Caterpillar Field
    Mechanic in Alaska." Clark College Foundation.
    Retrieved September 25, 2017. https://www
    .clarkcollegefoundation.org/captain.
mikeroweWORKS Foundation. "Justin Britton: Auto and
    Industrial Diesel Technician." March 23, 2016. http://

profoundlydisconnected.com
/justinbrittonworkethicscholarshipstory.

mikeroweWORKS Foundation. "Success Story: Jason
Surfling, 2013 AED Scholarship Recipient." April 14,
2014. http://profoundlydisconnected.com/jason
-surfling.

National Automotive Technicians Education Foundation.
"Career Tips." Retrieved September 25, 2017.
http://www.natef.org/NATEF-and-You/Students
-Parents/Career-Tips.aspx.

National Automotive Technicians Education Foundation.
"Realize Your Dream: Become a Truck Technician!"
Retrieved September 25, 2017. http://www.natef.org
/gctattachment/NATEF-and-You/Students-Parents
/Medium-Heavy-Truck/ase_career_truck.pdf.aspx.

National Institute for Automotive Service Excellence.
"About ASE." Retrieved September 25, 2017.
http://www.ase.com/About-ASE.aspx.

Phelps, Nathan. "Thinning Pool of Auto, Diesel Repair
Technicians." *Green Bay Press-Gazette*, March 20, 2015.
http://www.greenbaypressgazette.com/story/money
/companies/state-of-opportunity/2015/03/20/thinning
-pool-auto-diesel-repair-technicians/25110309.

Pool, Colton. "West Fargo Pioneer: GES, NDSCS Program
Gives Students Experience, Financial Aid." North
Dakota State College of Science. Retrieved September
25, 2017. https://www.ndscs.edu/news_events
/news/9324.

Southwest Wisconsin Workforce Development Board. "Craig Bunker Finds Success as Diesel Mechanic." Retrieved September 25, 2017. http://www.swwdb.org /success/BunkerC.html.

Wernie, Bradford. "High Demand for Diesel Techs." Automotive News, November 5, 2012.http://www. autonews.com/article/20121105 /RETAIL07/311059989/high-demand-for-diesel-techs

Western Tech. "Graduate Success: Fidel Gonzalez." Retrieved September 25, 2017. https://www .westerntech.edu/success-stories/graduate-success-fidel -gonzalez.

INDEX

A

Accrediting Commission of Career Schools and Colleges of Technology, 49

Accrediting Council for Independent Colleges and Schools, 49

aerospace, 33

alternative fuel, 16, 30

American Boat and Yacht Council (ABYC), 61

apprenticeship, 42

aptitude, 21, 27

Armed Services Vocational Aptitude Battery, 56

Association of Diesel Specialists (ADS), 30, 62–63

Automotive News, 33

B

boiler, 14

Boyce, Nancy, 21, 28

Britton, Justin, 39

Bureau of Labor Statistics (BLS), 63, 66

C

Caterpillar, 28, 39, 50, 51, 62

certificate, 39, 45

Clarion, The, 23

Clark College Foundation, 23, 28

clean diesel, 30, 31

College of Alameda, 51

computer systems, 14, 19, 29, 23, 27, 31, 34, 35, 63

Cummins, 50

D

Department of Education, 49

dexterity, 21

diagnostics, 20, 23, 27, 31, 33

drills, 23

drive train, 14, 60

E

economy, 11, 12, 63

electrical systems, 9, 14, 16, 23, 34, 60, 61

emission control, 10, 14, 19, 31, 32, 63

examinations, 16, 57, 58–62

F

farm equipment, 23

Firehouse, 32

flammable materials, 19

force, 34

Ford, 62

fossil fuel, 30

Freightliner, 28

friction, 34

G

General Education Development, GED, 43

General Equipment and Supplies, 55

generator, 14, 19, 25, 28, 32

ABOUT THE AUTHOR

Jennifer Culp is an author of nonfiction science and technology books for young adults.

PHOTO CREDITS

Cover, p. 3 Kot500/Shutterstock.com; pp. 6–7 Carolyn Franks/Shutterstock.com; p. 8 iNerus/Shutterstock.com; p. 12 Greg K_ca/Shutterstock.com; p. 13 santypan/Shutterstock.com; p. 17 donvictorio/Shutterstock.com; p. 19 Westend61/Getty Images; p. 22 Clerkenwell/Vetta/Getty Images; p. 24 Corepics VOF/Shutterstock.com; p. 27 aSuruwataRi/Shutterstock.com; p. 30 © iStockphoto.com/Pawel_Czaja; p. 32 BrandyTaylor/E+/Getty Images; p. 35 SolStock/E+/Getty Images; p. 36 XiXinXing/Shutterstock.com; p. 38 tdub303/E+/Getty Images; p. 41 JohnnyGreig/E+/Getty Images; p. 43 Monkey Business Images/Shutterstock.com; p. 46 Thomas Barwick/Taxi/Getty Images; p. 50 Ermolaev Alexander/Shutterstock.com; p. 51 jpgfactory/E+/Getty Images; p. 53 U.S. Navy photo by Bruce Cummins/Released; p. 58 Juanmonino/E+/Getty Images; p. 60 kali9/E+/Getty Images; p. 65 Gary Gershoff/WireImage /Getty Images; interior pages background (car engine) fuyu liu/Shutterstock.com.

Design: Nelson Sá; Layout: Nicole Russo-Duca; Editor: Phil Wolny; Photo Researcher: Karen Huang